✕

DEALING

WITH

DIFFICULT

PEOPLE

WITHOUT KILLING THEM

✕

MIKE D. ROBERTSON

STUDY GUIDE

Scripture quotations marked KJV are taken from the King James Version of the Bible. Public domain. Scripture quotations marked NIV are taken from the Holy Bible, New International Version®, NIV®. Copyright © 1973, 1978, 1984, 2011 by Biblica, Inc.™ Used by permission of Zondervan. All rights reserved worldwide. www.zondervan.com. The "NIV" and "New International Version" are trademarks registered in the United States Patent and Trademark Office by Biblica, Inc.™ | Scripture quotations marked NKJV are taken from the New King James Version®. Copyright © 1982 by Thomas Nelson. Used by permission. All rights reserved. | Scripture quotations marked TLB are taken from The Living Bible copy- right © 1971 by Tyndale House Foundation. Used by permission of Tyndale House Publishers Inc., Carol Stream, Illinois 60188. All rights reserved. The Living Bible, TLB, and The Living Bible logo are registered trademarks of Tyndale House Publishers. | Scripture quotations marked NLT are taken from the Holy Bible, New Living Translation, copyright © 1996, 2004, 2015 by Tyndale House Foundation. Used by permission of Tyndale House Publishers, Inc., Carol Stream, Illinois 60188. All rights reserved. | Scripture quotations marked MSG are taken from THE MESSAGE, copyright © 1993, 1994, 1995, 1996, 2000, 2001, 2002 by Eugene H. Peterson. Used by permission of NavPress. All rights reserved. Represented by Tyndale House Publishers, Inc. | Scripture quotations marked GNT are from the Good News Translation in Today's English Version—Second Edition. Copyright © 1992 by American Bible Society. Used by Permission.

For foreign and subsidiary rights, contact the author.

Interior Photos: © Shutterstock, Andrew van Tilborgh, Jessica Hegland, Dominic Fondon

ISBN: 978-1-950718-46-7   1 2 3 4 5 6 7 8 9 10

Printed in the United States of America

×

DEALING

WITH

DIFFICULT

PEOPLE

WITHOUT KILLING THEM

×

MIKE D. ROBERTSON

STUDY GUIDE

CONTENTS

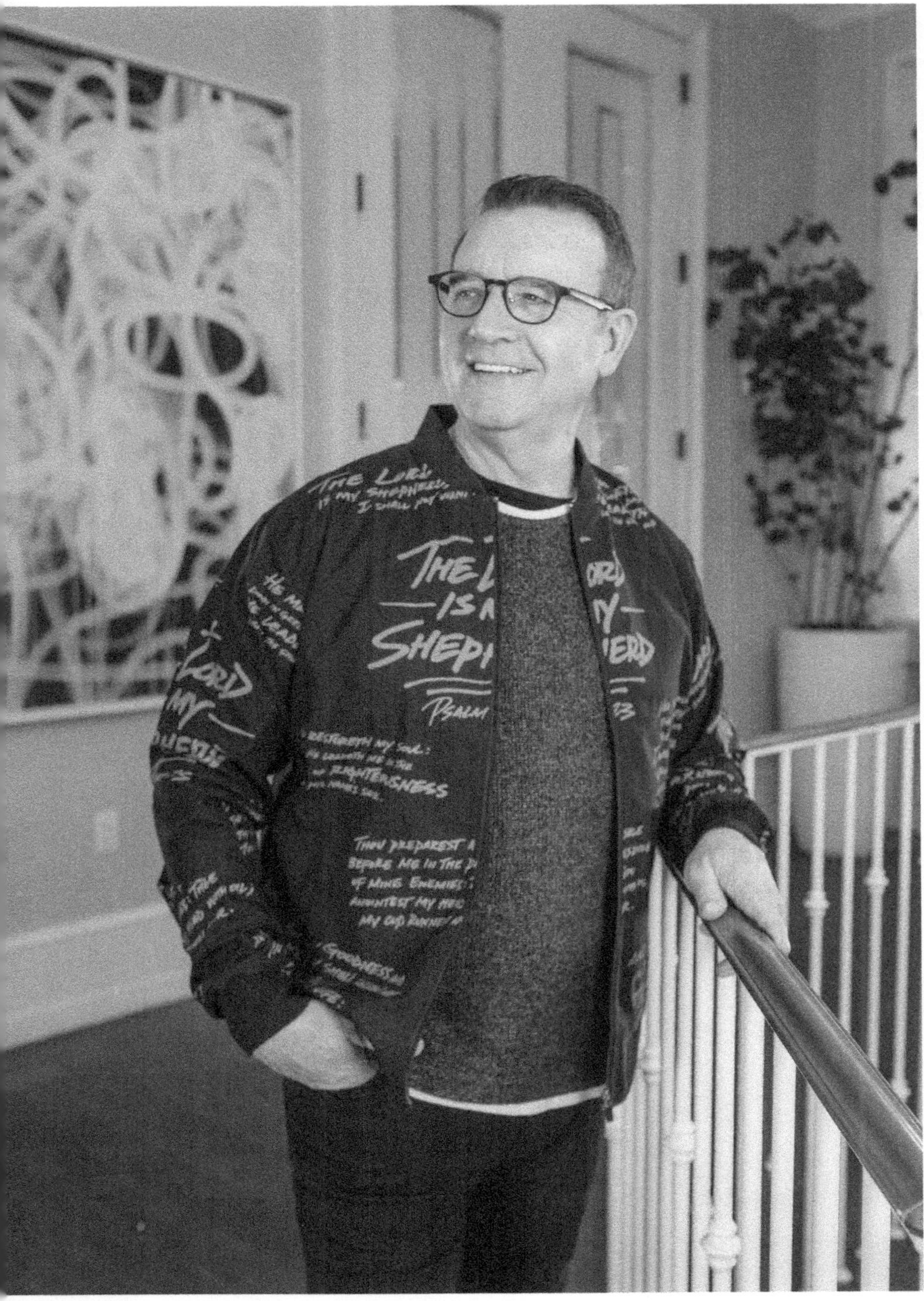

The Hidden Blessings of a Jackass

○ ○ ○

"Wherever we encounter them, difficult people can play an important part in our lives if we will let them. Sometimes we must face an adversary if we are to rise up to the next level God has for us, whether that's in church leadership, in business, or in our homes."

READ / Introduction

O O O

READING TIME

Read the Introduction in Dealing with Difficult People. Use the Notes space to record any thoughts you want to remember or questions you want to talk about later.

O O O

OPENING THOUGHTS /

Why do you think our culture has the expectation that relationships (and life in general) are meant to exist without conflict or difficulty?

_____

_____

_____

_____

_____

_____

Have you seen God bring good out of a relationship difficulty in your life? How so?

_____

_____

_____

_____

_____

_____

RESPOND /

How was Judas's betrayal essential to Jesus's journey to the cross? How might the difficult people in your life be essential to God's purpose for you?

_____

_____

_____

_____

_____

What can we learn about dealing with difficult people from the way Jesus deals with Judas in this passage (and even throughout their three-year friendship prior to this moment)?

_____

_____

_____

_____

_____

What's the danger of expecting salvation—or relationships—to be free of any hardship? How could this hinder our faith and maturity??

_____

_____

_____

_____

_____

○ ○ ○

STUDY SCRIPTURE

Read Matthew 26:47-50.

"While he was still speaking, Judas came, one of the twelve, and with him a great crowd with swords and clubs, from the chief priests and the elders of the people. Now the betrayer had given them a sign, saying, 'The one I will kiss is the man; seize him.' And he came up to Jesus at once and said, 'Greetings, Rabbi!' And he kissed him. Jesus said to him, 'Friend, do what you came to do.' Then they came up and laid hands on Jesus and seized him."

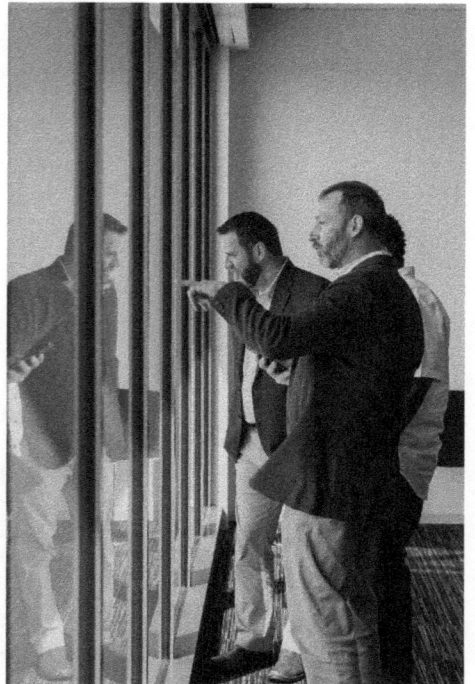

○ ○ ○

What aspects of our culture reinforce the belief that things should come easily and cheaply for us?

_____

_____

_____

_____

_____

Have you ever tried to run from a difficult relationship instead of facing the issues? If so, how did that situation work out for you?

_____

_____

_____

_____

_____

_____

In the introduction, Pastor Mike looks at the lives of Joseph, David, and Jesus as examples of people who took difficult relationships and allowed God to grow them in the midst of that conflict. Can you think of any other Biblical stories where this is also the case?

_____

_____

_____

_____

_____

_____

○ ○ ○

In your own words, what does it mean to "take the rough with the smooth" when it comes to the people in your life?

_____

_____

_____

_____

How have difficult people made you a better person? What specific ways have you grown because of conflict and differences?

_____

_____

_____

_____

How do you think leaders can practically prepare to deal with more conflict and difficult people than the average person?

_____

_____

_____

_____

CHAPTER 1

Rooted in Relationships

○ ○ ○

"Whether we like it or not, we all need others, to help make us more who God intends for us to be. We have to be rooted in relationships with others if we are to really grow in God."

READ / Chapter 1

○ ○ ○

OPENING THOUGHTS /

Why do you think God wired us in such a way that we need other people? What does this say about his nature?

_____

_____

_____

_____

_____

_____

READING TIME

Read Chapter 1 in Dealing with Difficult People. Use the Notes space to record any thoughts you want to remember or questions you want to talk about later.

How have other people—especially other believers—in your life helped to balance out your personal weaknesses?

_____

_____

_____

_____

_____

_____

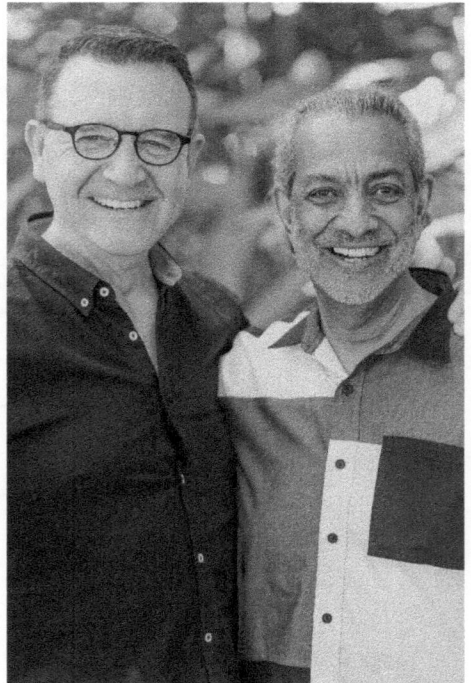

○ ○ ○

STUDY SCRIPTURE

Read Genesis 2:18-24

"Then the LORD God said, 'It is not good that the man should be alone; I will make him a helper fit for him.' Now out of the ground the LORD God had formed every beast of the field and every bird of the heavens and brought them to the man to see what he would call them. And whatever the man called every living creature, that was its name. The man gave names to all livestock and to the birds of the heavens and to every beast of the field.

But for Adam there was not found a helper fit for him. So the LORD God caused a deep sleep to fall upon the man, and while he slept took one of his ribs and closed up its place with flesh. And the rib that the LORD God had taken from the man he made into a woman and brought her to the man. Then the man said,

'This at last is bone of my bones
    and flesh of my flesh;
she shall be called Woman,
    because she was taken out of Man.'

Therefore a man shall leave his father and his mother and hold fast to his wife, and they shall become one flesh. And the man and his wife were both naked and were not ashamed."

RESPOND /

Why do you think God was the first one to say that Adam shouldn't be alone? Why is it important that it was him, and not Adam, who declared this?

_____

_____

_____

_____

_____

Even in paradise—in a perfect world—Adam needed a companion. What does this reveal about our needs in a fallen, broken world?

_____

_____

_____

_____

Why do those who recognize that they are sinners usually have an easier time showing grace to others?

_____

_____

_____

_____

○ ○ ○

REFLECT AND DISCUSS /

Proverbs 27:17 says, "As iron sharpens iron, so one person sharpens another."

Think about the five closest people in your life. Are they making you better, or pulling you backwards? How do you know?

_____

_____

_____

_____

In your own words, what's the difference between someone who makes you uncomfortable and someone who is difficult?

_____

_____

_____

_____

○ ○ ○

Of the four types of relationships discussed in this chapter, which one describes the majority of your current relationships? Why do you think this is?

_____

_____

_____

_____

Have you ever had to let go of a "friend for a season"? What was difficult about this process? Did it have any benefits?

_____

_____

_____

_____

In your own words, explain why clear expectations in each relationship are so important to the health of that relationship.

_____

_____

_____

_____

Have you ever had a "friend of treason"? Did God use this person to bring about any good in your life, even indirectly?

_____

_____

_____

_____

You Can't Keep Running

○ ○ ○

"As a leader, Paul knew that it was not healthy to let difficult people continue in their ways without dealing with the problem. It remains true: we can't afford to ignore difficult people just because we are not directly involved or affected. They will have a negative impact on others we are responsible for, if we just leave things as they are. This is one reason anyone in leadership will have need to know how to deal with difficult people."

○ ○ ○

READ / Chapter 2

○ ○ ○

READING TIME

Read Chapter 2 in Dealing with Difficult People. Use the Notes space to record any thoughts you want to remember or questions you want to talk about later.

○ ○ ○

OPENING THOUGHTS /

What cost does running from a difficult relationship (or even a difficult community) have, in your opinion?

_____

_____

_____

_____

_____

_____

How have you seen grace and understanding change, or even eliminate, the tension between two people?

_____

_____

_____

_____

_____

_____

STUDY SCRIPTURE

Read Philemon 10-16

"I appeal to you for my child, Onesimus, whose father I became in my imprisonment. (Formerly he was useless to you, but now he is indeed useful to you and to me.) I am sending him back to you, sending my very heart. I would have been glad to keep him with me, in order that he might serve me on your behalf during my imprisonment for the gospel, but I preferred to do nothing without your consent in order that your goodness might not be by compulsion but of your own accord.

For this perhaps is why he was parted from you for a while, that you might have him back forever, no longer as a bondservant but more than a bondservant, as a beloved brother—especially to me, but how much more to you, both in the flesh and in the Lord."

RESPOND /

How does Paul's tone in this letter promote unity and understanding between all three parties involved? What difference does your tone make when you're talking with difficult people?

_____

_____

_____

_____

THOU PREPAREST
BEFORE ME IN THE
OF MINE ENEMIES
ANOINTEST MY
MY CUP RUNNETH
GOODNESS AND
Y SHALL FOLLOW ME
ALL THE
DAYS OF MY LIFE:

Why did Paul insist that Philemon and Onesimus's spiritual bond come before their natural disputes? Does this change your perspective at all on conflicts you may have with other believers?

_____

_____

_____

Why do you think Pastor Mike asserts that the way you deal with difficult people says more about your faith than how much Bible you can quote, or how often you attend church? Why is handling conflict a better display of your spiritual fruit?

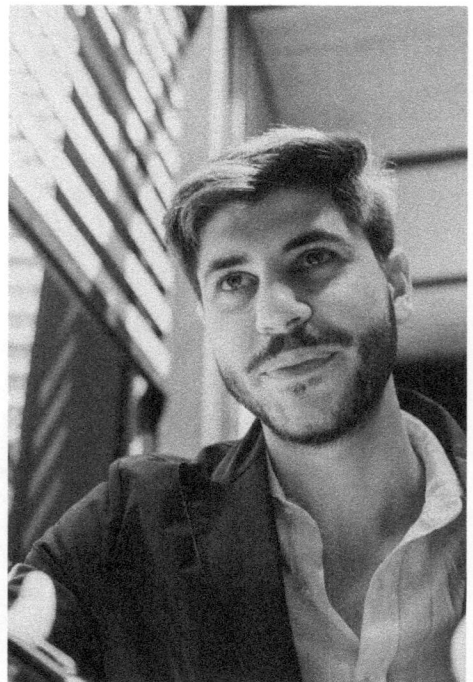

_____

_____

_____

Think of a time you struggled with unforgiveness towards another person. How did unforgiveness hurt and hinder you?

_____

_____

_____

_____

_____

SHARE YOUR STORY

"Running away isn't a long-term solution. While it might be right for us to put distance between us and someone or something at a certain stage, likely there will come a day when it is time to go back."

How can you extend grace and understanding to a difficult person who is currently in your life? What might this look like practically?

_____

_____

_____

_____

_____

Pastor Mike makes the point that our heart when it comes to our relationship with God—and our relationships with others—is more important than our deeds. What negative impact might good deeds alone—with no real heart behind them—have on both ourselves and others?

_____

_____

_____

_____

_____

○ ○ ○

Have you ever encountered a relationship in which reconciliation wasn't possible? What did you learn from this experience?

_____

_____

_____

How has this chapter shifted your viewpoint on the most important aspects of a relationship between two believers? Do you sense God shifting your priorities to align more with his own? If so, how?

_____

_____

_____

Why is a strong relationship with God always the starting point to strong, healthy relationships with other people?

_____

_____

_____

The Rhythms and Rules of Relationships

○ ○ ○

"When we understand the way in which relationships are intended to flourish, we may be able to identify which parts of that process may have been missed or cut short with that difficult person."

READ / Chapter 3

READING TIME

Read Chapter 3 in Dealing with Difficult People. Use the Notes space to record any thoughts you want to remember or questions you want to talk about later.

OPENING THOUGHTS /

In your own perspective, what role do expectations play in conflict and disappointment? How can bad expectations set a relationship up for tension?

_____

_____

_____

_____

_____

What possible dangers are there in a relationship that develops too quickly, or one in which people begin to share deep, confidential information too fast?

_____

_____

_____

_____

_____

STUDY SCRIPTURE

Read Matthew 7:16-20.

"By their fruit you will recognize them. Do people pick grapes from thornbushes, or figs from thistles? Likewise, every good tree bears good fruit, but a bad tree bears bad fruit. A good tree cannot bear bad fruit, and a bad tree cannot bear good fruit. Every tree that does not bear good fruit is cut down and thrown into the fire. Thus, by their fruit you will recognize them."

RESPOND /

Pastor Mike writes, "Wonderful fruit can come in odd-looking shapes." Why do you think this is? How might "odd" character traits actually be the very qualities we need in a brother or sister in Christ?

_____

_____

_____

_____

_____

How have you seen the good fruit of those in your life benefit you? How has God used your good fruit to benefit your family and friends?

_____

_____

_____

_____

_____

Why do you think it's so important for people to be tended to in relationships?

_____

_____

_____

_____

_____

How can a better understanding of how relationships grow and develop help protect us from an abundance of difficult people in our lives?

_____

_____

_____

_____

_____

Has a difficult person ever caused you to treat others less well? If so, what happened?

_____

_____

_____

_____

Pastor Mike writes, "Nabal brought out the fighter in David; Abigail brought out the king in him. Nabal provoked a reactionary spirit; Abigail promoted a royalty attitude." What kind of attitude are you fostering in those you love? How can you bring out the best in them?

_____

_____

_____

_____

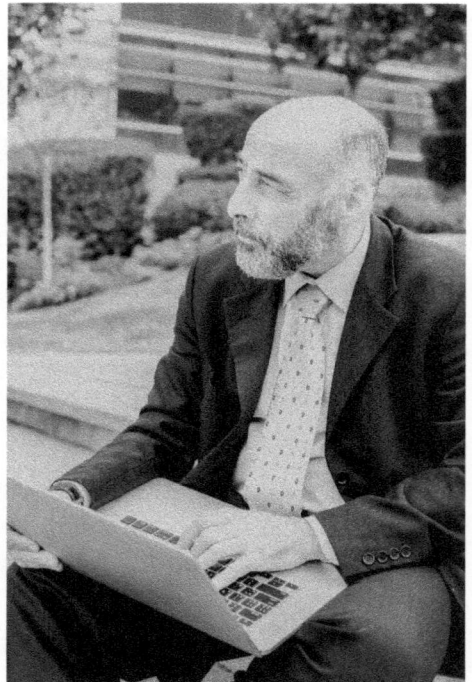

○ ○ ○

In your own words, what's the difference between authenticity and transparency?

_____

_____

_____

Have you ever been too transparent with another person (or has another person ever been too transparent with you)? What was the result?

_____

_____

_____

Why is character so essential to any relationship? What would happen in a relationship devoid of character?

_____

_____

_____

It's Time to Let Them Go

○ ○ ○

"I have found over the years that there seems to be a real correlation between the amount of time someone spends in the Bible and their capacity for being easily ticked off by something or someone. I believe that's because the more we allow God's Word to sink into our hearts, the less room there will be for offenses."

READ / Chapter 4

READING TIME

Read Chapter 4 in Dealing with Difficult People. Use the Notes space to record any thoughts you want to remember or questions you want to talk about later.

OPENING THOUGHTS /

Is there ever a good or right time to be offended? If so, when?

_____

_____

_____

_____

_____

What role does our perspective play in how long we remain offended? How can a right perspective keep us from staying offended too long?

_____

_____

_____

_____

_____

RESPOND /

What did Jesus mean in this passage by the word "offended"? What kind of reaction to the message of the gospel is he referring to here?

_____

_____

_____

_____

_____

Why do you think offense in the church is so surprising and painful for us? How could our own false expectations contribute to this discomfort?

_____

_____

_____

_____

_____

Why do you think leaving a wound, or offense, unaddressed causes it to fester and grow?

_____

_____

_____

_____

_____

STUDY SCRIPTURE

Read Matthew 11:4-6.

"Go and tell John the things which you hear and see: The blind see and the lame walk; the lepers are cleansed and the deaf hear; the dead are raised up and the poor have the gospel preached to them. And blessed is he who is not offended because of Me."

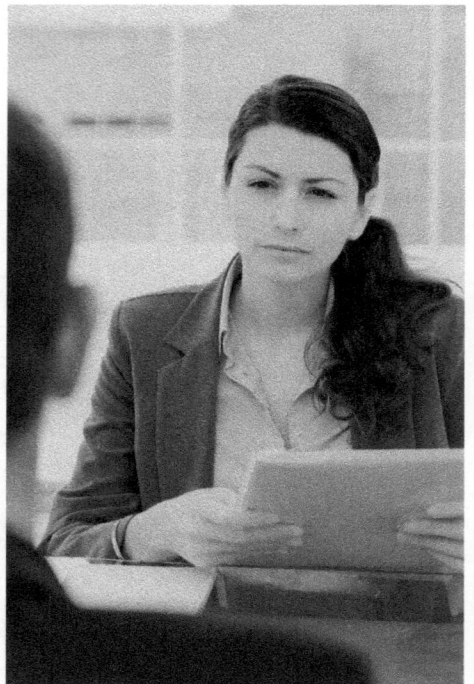

○ ○ ○

How can we begin to have a more realistic perspective of our relationships—especially with other believers? How might this save us heartache down the road?

_____

_____

_____

_____

_____

○ ○ ○

SHARE YOUR STORY

"The real problem here is not what someone may have said or done to you, it's how you choose to respond."

Can you recall a time or two when Jesus was offended? How did he handle it? What example does this provide for us?

_____

_____

_____

_____

_____

What opportunities for growth might be hiding inside an offense (growth for both ourselves and the other person)?

_____

_____

_____

_____

_____

○ ○ ○

Think about someone you're currently in conflict with, or someone with whom you had a recent conflict. Did you spend more time complaining about the situation, or focusing on what God was going to do? What power do you think your words had over the situation?

_____

_____

_____

Why do you think the enemy is aiming for the church to be in constant conflict and strife with one another? What repercussions does this have within the church? Outside of it?

_____

_____

_____

How have you seen grace and gentleness completely turn a conflict around? Why do you think it's so impactful?

_____

_____

_____

CHAPTER 5

The Wound of Betrayal

○ ○ ○

"Are there situations you are ignoring or avoiding because they seem too awkward to deal with, or because they strike too close to home? Pretending they are not there may make it feel like they have gone away for a time, but one day they are likely to "come back"—or, really, just reappear—and bite you."

○ ○ ○

READ / Chapter 5

○ ○ ○

○ ○ ○

READING TIME

Read Chapter 5 in Dealing with Difficult People. Use the Notes space to record any thoughts you want to remember or questions you want to talk about later.

OPENING THOUGHTS /

Why do you think it's hard for many people to accept that they can't control others' words and actions?

_____

_____

_____

_____

_____

Where we find our identity makes a huge dif- ference in how offended we become. When we find our identity in God, how does it change the way we respond to those who treat us poorly?

_____

_____

_____

_____

_____

○ ○ ○

STUDY SCRIPTURE

Read Hebrews 13:15-19.

"Through him then let us continually offer up a sacrifice of praise to God, that is, the fruit of lips that acknowledge his name. Do not neglect to do good and to share what you have, for such sacrifices are pleasing to God.

Obey your leaders and submit to them, for they are keeping watch over your souls, as those who will have to give an account. Let them do this with joy and not with groaning, for that would be of no advantage to you.

Pray for us, for we are sure that we have a clear conscience, desiring to act honorably in all things. I urge you the more earnestly to do this in order that I may be restored to you the sooner."

RESPOND /

Pastor Mike writes, "Honor is about the office God has established, not the person." How does this perspective change the way in which we honor our leaders?

_____

_____

_____

_____

When believers respond to conflict in an un-Christ-like manner, how does it affect our witness? How does it affect the church's reputation?

_____

_____

_____

_____

Pastor Mike writes, "Honor is about the office God has established, not the person." How does this perspective change the way in which we honor our leaders?

_____

_____

_____

_____

When believers respond to conflict in an un-Christ-like manner, how does it affect our witness? How does it affect the church's reputation?

_____

_____

_____

_____

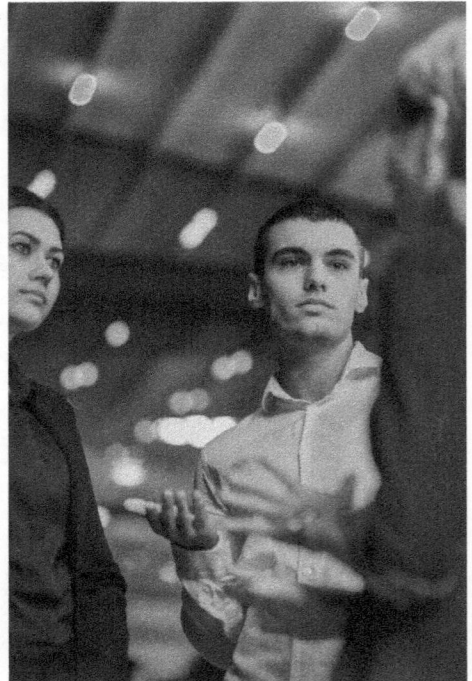

○ ○ ○

Typically, how do you respond to a situation you can't control? What's your natural reaction? Do you try to take matters into your own hands?

_____

_____

_____

How can it actually be beneficial for us to learn how to "lose" an argument, or endure defeat?

_____

_____

_____

Our response to conflict is just as important as the words of the other person. How can our words add fuel to the fire? How can our words soothe and calm the situation?

_____

_____

_____

According to this chapter, what's the difference between prayer and confession? How do they work together in our communication with God?

_____

_____

_____

Forgiveness is a verb. What are some practical ways you can demonstrate forgiveness to someone, even when you don't feel like it?

_____

_____

_____

What risks do we run when we try to sweep offenses under the carpet and ignore them? How does this actually hurt us in the long run?

_____

_____

_____

According to Scripture, what should be our first response when others offend us? What are some concrete ways you can live this out in your own life?

_____

_____

_____

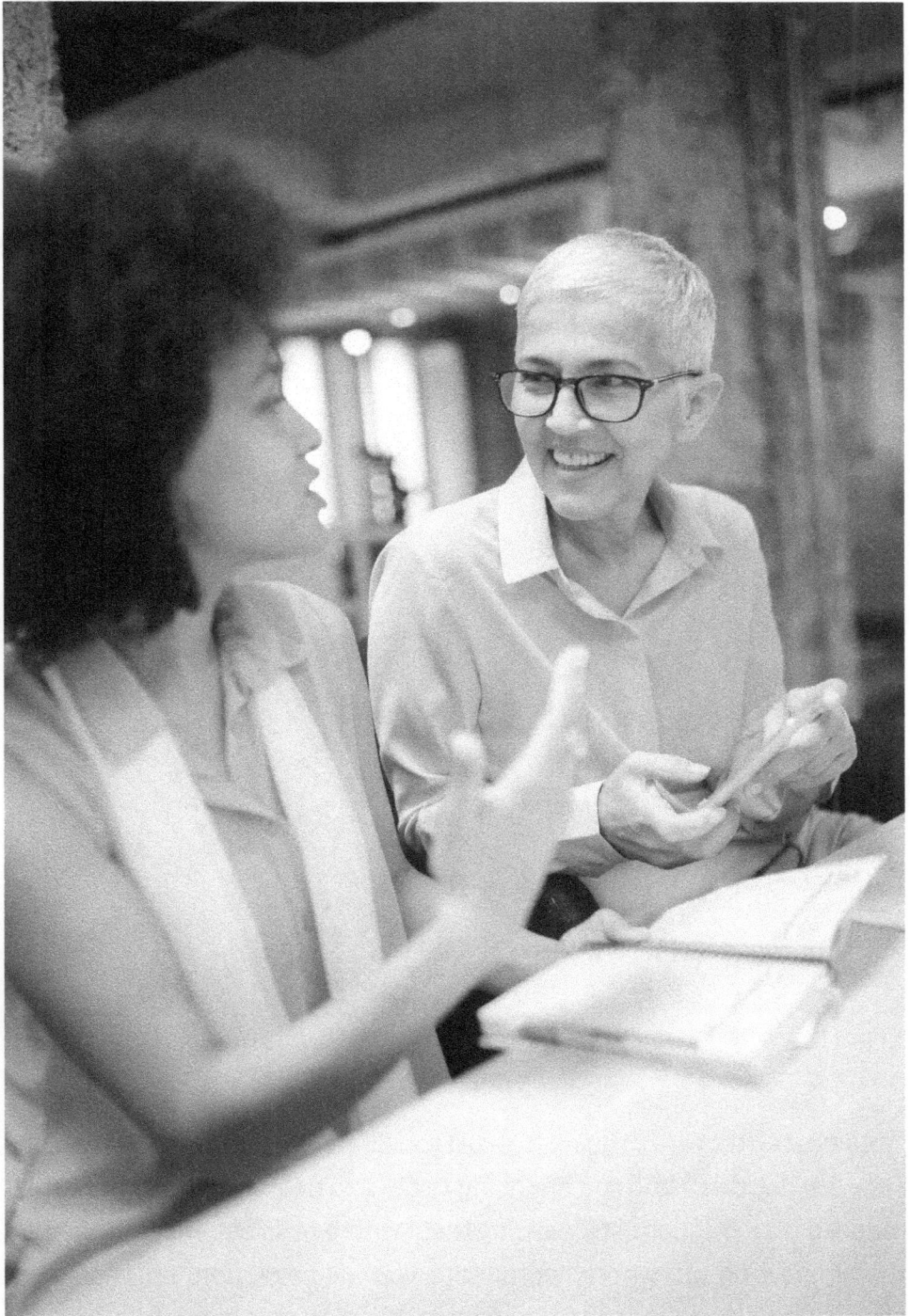

Dealing With Difficult People

○ ○ ○

"Your best efforts aren't going to make your life a difficult-person-free-zone. They are out there and you are going to have to deal with them. But having reduced their frequency by avoiding them where possible, and downgrading their impact on you where appropriate, you will have more emotional and spiritual capacity to face those you must. It's all in your hands."

READ / Chapter 6

○ ○ ○

READING TIME

Read Chapter 6 in Dealing with Difficult People. Use the Notes space to record any thoughts you want to remember or questions you want to talk about later.

○ ○ ○

OPENING THOUGHTS /

How can we rejuvenate and recover after dealing with a difficult person? What are some specific things you like to do?

_____

_____

_____

_____

_____

Why is it important to lean on other leaders to help you deal with difficult people? Have you ever tried to deal with all the difficult people in your life by yourself? What was the result?

_____

_____

_____

_____

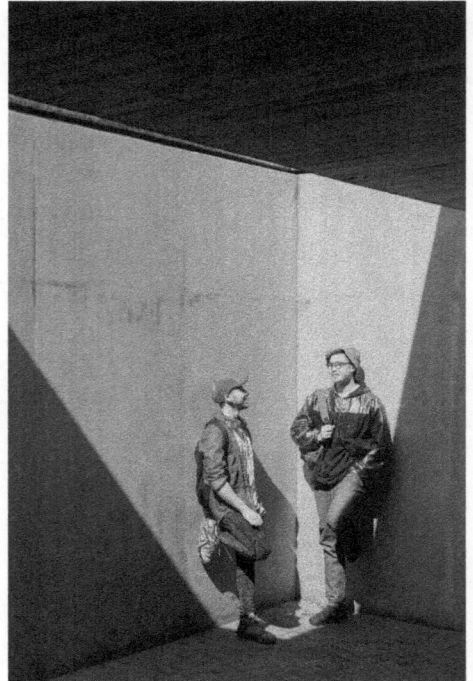

STUDY SCRIPTURE

Read 2 Corinthians 10:3-5.

"For though we walk in the flesh, we are not waging war according to the flesh. For the weapons of our warfare are not of the flesh but have divine power to destroy strong-holds. We destroy arguments and every lofty opinion raised against the knowledge of God, and take every thought captive to obey Christ, being ready to punish every disobedience, when your obedi-ence is complete."

RESPOND /

Out of the six groups of difficult people Pastor Mike outlined, which stands out the most to you? Why do you think this is?

_____

_____

_____

_____

What role does our own "self-counsel," or self-talk, play in our response to difficult people?

_____

_____

_____

_____

Why do you think Proverbs 18:21 says, "The tongue has the power of life and death?" How have you seen the tongue bring death? What about life?

_____

_____

_____

_____

○ ○ ○

What gifts do you have that stand apart from the rest? What makes you unique? How can you use that gift to serve God and others?

_____

_____

_____

_____

○ ○ ○

SHARE YOUR STORY

"The problem is not the problem—the problem is what we think about the problem. If we can change our thoughts, we can change our feelings about situations— and people."

Think about the "true, noble, right, pure, lovely, admirable" things in your life. What can you thank God for today? How does this change your perspective on the negative things in your life?

_____

_____

_____

_____

How can we find power in "seeking to understand" more than we seek to be understood? How does this affect the other person in the relationship?

_____

_____

_____

_____

Do you find saying "no" to others easy? Why or why not? Can you recall a time that Jesus said no? What purpose did his "no" serve?

_____

_____

_____

Now that you understand the categories of difficult people more clearly, does it help shed some light on why the difficult people in your life act and speak the way they do? What do you better understand about them?

_____

_____

_____

Take a few minutes to pray through this prayer from St. Francis of Assisi, surrendering your heart to the Lord, and asking him to make it like his own:

Lord, make me an instrument of your peace;
where there is hatred, let me sow love;
where there is injury, pardon;
where there is discord, union;
where there is doubt, faith;
where there is despair, hope;
where there is darkness, light;
and where there is sadness, joy.

The Power of Love

o o o

"You can know exactly what you should do and give it your best shot, but without accessing the power that is available to you, there's no way you can be successful in your own strength."

READ / Chapter 7

○ ○ ○

OPENING THOUGHTS /

Why do you think so many people have a harder time loving themselves than loving others?

_____

_____

_____

_____

How does society define the word "love"? How do you define it? How does the Bible define it? Why do you think we have so many differing definitions of love?

_____

_____

_____

_____

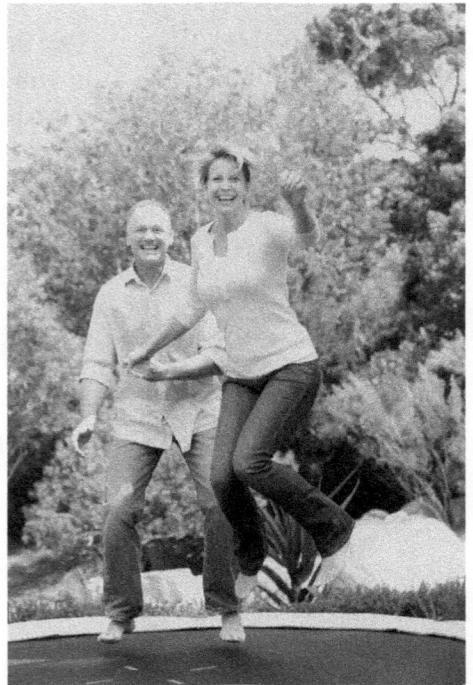

○ ○ ○

STUDY SCRIPTURE

Read Luke 6:27-36.

"But to you who are listening I say: Love your enemies, do good to those who hate you, bless those who curse you, pray for those who mistreat you. If someone slaps you on one cheek, turn to them the other also. If someone takes your coat, do not withhold your shirt from them. Give to everyone who asks you, and if anyone takes what belongs to you, do not demand it back.

Do to others as you would have them do to you. If you love those who love you, what credit is that to you? Even sinners love those who love them. And if you do good to those who are good to you, what credit is that to you? Even sinners do that. And if you lend to those from whom you expect repayment, what credit is that to you? Even sinners lend to sinners, expecting to be repaid in full.

RESPOND /

What confidence or security do we need in order to be okay with others not paying us back? What inner strength does this require?

_____

_____

_____

SHARE YOUR STORY

"What sets agape love apart from the three others— phileo, storge, eros—is that it is not based on feelings. The three involve me feeling something: friendly, family, or frisky. Agape is all about God and his actions for and in me. It's love as a verb."

How might others' failure to respond in kind actually help us grow and mature? Have you experienced a situation in which someone let you down, and it actually made you a better person?

_____

_____

_____

_____

In your own words, explain the differences between the four kinds of love. Which type of love characterizes most of your relationships? Why do you say that?

_____

_____

_____

_____

Why do we first need to experience God's agape love before we can show it to others?

_____

_____

_____

_____

Jesus introduced Peter to agape love during his time on earth; but he refined Peter's sense of agape love during Peter's own ministry experience. Why do you think God used people in this process?

_____

_____

_____

Our culture elevates and almost worships eros love. Why do you think this is? How does this shortchange the true meaning of love?

_____

_____

_____

Do you truly believe that, as Pastor Mike writes, "we are meant to enjoy life, not just endure it"? If so, what helped you come to this place in your perspective? If not, what's holding you back?

_____

_____

_____

How can our reactions to difficult people teach others about agape love? What does this require us to give up, or sacrifice?

_____

_____

_____

What's the number one personal action step you want to take away from this study? What is God calling you to change in your life right now as it relates to relationships and difficult people? Write a short prayer asking for his help in being obedient to this action step.

_____

_____

_____

_____

_____

_____

_____

_____

_____

www.ingramcontent.com/pod-product-compliance
Lightning Source LLC
Chambersburg PA
CBHW020217090426
42734CB00008B/1109